Zeitgeist 2
OCR

Self Study Guide

Miriam Friedmann

OXFORD
UNIVERSITY PRESS

OXFORD
UNIVERSITY PRESS

Great Clarendon Street, Oxford OX2 6DP

Oxford University Press is a department of the University of Oxford.
It furthers the University's objective of excellence in research, scholarship,
and education by publishing worldwide in

Oxford New York
Auckland Cape Town Dar es Salaam Hong Kong Karachi
Kuala Lumpur Madrid Melbourne Mexico City Nairobi
New Delhi Shanghai Taipei Toronto

With offices in

Argentina Austria Brazil Chile Czech Republic France Greece
Guatemala Hungary Italy Japan South Korea Poland Portugal
Singapore Switzerland Thailand Turkey Ukraine Vietnam

Oxford is a registered trade mark of Oxford University Press
in the UK and in certain other countries

British Library Cataloguing in Publication Data

Data available

ISBN 978 019 915401 2

1 3 5 7 9 10 8 6 4 2

Printed in Great Britain by by Ashford Colour Press Ltd.

Acknowledgements

The author and publisher would like to thank Melissa Weir (project
manager), Deborah Manning (editor), and Marion Dill (language
consultant).

Contents

Here's a reminder of the topics from the OCR A2 specification which you need to revise for the examination. These are the topic and sub-topic headings, but you can find more detail on each if you consult the specification.

Society
Integration and exclusion – Law and order – Unemployment

Environment
The individual and the environment – Energy management – Pollution – Conservation of the natural world

Science and technology
Medical progress – Scientific advances – Technological developments

Culture
Literature and the arts – Political issues – Heritage and history

You will be taking two examinations:

A2 Unit 3: Speaking

The Speaking Test is worth 15% of your A Level.

The test lasts 15 minutes and you have 20 minutes to prepare beforehand.

You are not allowed to use a dictionary.

There are two sections:
  Discussion of an article in German (5–6 minutes)
  Discussing one or two sub-topics of your choice from the list above (10–12 minutes)

A2 Unit 4: Listening, Reading and Writing

This paper is worth 35% of your A Level and the time allowed is two hours and forty-five minutes.

There are three sections:
  Listening and Writing
  Reading and Writing
  Writing

Remember that your AS grade represents 50% of your A Level.

Pass grades for this examination range from A* and A down to E.

The descriptions of what you need to be able to do are very similar to those at AS Level, **but remember that this is in the context of the more demanding texts and tasks which you will meet at A2.** Two new things which are expected are an ability to transfer meaning from German into English accurately and an ability to cope with the unpredictable when you are talking to someone. Here's a reminder of the other expectations:

If you pass A Level German with an A grade, it means you can:

▸ clearly understand spoken language, including details and opinions.
▸ work out what someone is trying to say even if they don't spell it out in detail.
▸ clearly understand written texts, understanding both the gist and the details.
▸ talk fluently, giving your opinions and justifying them, and using a good range of vocabulary and generally accurate pronunciation.
▸ organise your ideas and write them up well in German.
▸ write using a wide range of vocabulary and grammatical structures without making many mistakes.

If you pass A Level German with an E grade, it means you:

▸ show some understanding of spoken German, even if you have difficulties when the language is complex and miss some of the details.
▸ can sometimes work out what someone is trying to say even if they don't give all the details.
▸ understand straightforward written texts, although you don't always understand more difficult writing.
▸ can talk in German, and convey basic information, perhaps a little hesitantly and relying on pre-learned material. There is probably some English influence on your pronunciation.
▸ can convey information in writing, perhaps with some difficulty in organising your material and expressing it.
▸ use a range of vocabulary and structures, but quite often you make mistakes.

Preparing for the exams

You can see from these lists that when planning your revision there are really six areas you need to practise:
Speaking – Listening – Reading – Writing – Vocabulary – Grammar

There are tips on how to prepare each area overleaf.

> Remember too that a knowledge of German or German-speaking culture is needed when you are discussing your chosen topic with the oral examiner or writing your essay for Unit 4. Do your research using articles written in German!

Speaking

▸ Take every opportunity to practise speaking German – in lessons, with the language assistant, with a friend, with anyone you know who speaks German.

▸ Revise all the topics (including AS topics!) you have studied thoroughly. Learn key vocabulary for each topic, using the lists which start on page 38 and your own notes.

▸ Practise discussing written texts, using the materials in the next section (page 9 onwards) and as many sample or past papers as you can find. You could also work with a partner, each taking a text and preparing suitable questions, then role-playing this section of the exam together.

▸ For the second section, choose two topics you can research in a German-speaking context and also have opinions and ideas on. Remember that you must show factual knowledge of these topics; make lists of questions which might be asked on each. Don't write everything out in full; note just a few key words down for reference, but definitely no full sentences.

Listening

▸ Keep listening to German, ideally every day. Use a mix of extracts you have worked on and new texts.

▸ Try listening to something for which you have the transcript. Just listen first, then listen again with the transcript and, if necessary, look up unknown words. Finally, listen again without the transcript and challenge yourself to understand everything.

▸ Watching films is excellent listening practice and watching more than once is even better! Try watching with the subtitles and then without. If you find this hard going, just re-watch a short extract.

▸ German radio and TV programmes are useful, but can also be difficult. Record an extract and listen or watch it more than once. You will find it gets easier.

▸ Make sure you do some exam listening practice too!

Reading

▸ Keep reading a mix of things you read once quickly, such as a magazine, and things where you work hard at a short passage and try to understand everything. Texts from your textbook are useful for this.

▸ It's useful to note new vocabulary from your reading, but don't make it such hard work that you give up. Note, say, three new words from each text.

▸ Try a 'dual-language' reading book, where you get the original German on one page and an English translation on the opposite one. This is an excellent way to practise reading longer texts without losing heart!

▸ Search on the internet for articles in German on any topic which interests you.

Writing

- As for the speaking test, a good knowledge of vocabulary for each topic is a must.
- Your examples and ideas should be based on Germany or a German-speaking country, so collect useful information on each topic from German sources.
- Practise planning essays – in German! – looking carefully at the question and sketching ideas for a **relevant** introduction, a series of paragraphs to develop the argument and a conclusion.
- Look carefully at marked work and identify what grammar errors you are making. Then check them in a grammar book and try some practice exercises.
- Make sure you are writing – and learning! – lists of key vocabulary for each of the two cultural topics. In addition, learn a good range of 'essay phrases' for introducing ideas, giving opinions, summing up and so on.

Vocabulary

- Learn lists of words regularly and build in time to go back over words you learned a week or two ago. Reinforcement makes them stick!
- Choose a system of recording new words which works for you. It could be paper lists, small sections on individual cards, recording the words and their English meanings on tape, making posters to stick on your bedroom wall ... what's important is that you are noting the words and going over them regularly!
- You were probably encouraged to use a good range of vocabulary in the essays you wrote during the year. Go back over them, highlighting good words and phrases and writing the English in the margin, then use this to test yourself. Words are often easier to learn in context.

Grammar

- Keep doing practice exercises in areas where you know you are weak.
- Use reading texts to practise thinking grammatically. For example, highlight a selection of adjectives, then write out the English for the phrases in which they appear. Test yourself by reproducing the German phrases accurately, complete with all the correct agreements!
- Keep learning from your verb tables until you know all the forms of each tense of regular verbs and the most common irregular verbs. Test yourself using a die. 1 = *ich*, 2 = *du*, 3 = *er/sie/es*, 4 = *wir*, 5 = *ihr*, 6 = *sie/Sie*. Use a verb list, choose an infinitive and a tense at random, throw the die and say the correct form of the verb. Practise until you can do it without hesitation.

The Speaking Test: what you need to know

The test has two parts: discussing a text and discussing one or two of the sub-topics you have studied (see the list on page 13).

Discussing a text (5–6 minutes)
You will have 20 minutes to prepare the text you are given.

> ‣ First, read the text carefully and decide what it is about. You need to know it well, so you can quickly identify which section the examiner's questions refer to.

> ‣ Try to predict what initial, factual questions you might be asked: *Was ist hier passiert? Wie hat X reagiert?* You might also be asked to explain a phrase in your own words.

> ‣ Decide what the themes of the text are, because the examiner will move onto a discussion of those – one idea will be given in the third bullet point, but you should also try to think of other related themes too. It might help to jot down key vocabulary for this section. Decide what you think, how you will express it and what you will say if the examiner questions your point of view.

To do well on this section you need to show a good understanding of the text and an ability to explain its themes and justify your opinions. You also need to show that you readily understand what the examiner says to you and respond appropriately, even to the unexpected. Quality of language is assessed too.

Discussing one or two sub-topics (10–12 minutes)
You will be asked to choose two sub-topics and to spend 10–12 minutes discussing the material you have researched. The emphasis here is on a depth of knowledge on your chosen aspect of the sub-topic. If the discussion on the first topic takes the full amount of time, you won't move onto the second topic.

Choose your two topics carefully and research a good range of material on each. For these two topics, be especially careful to collect plenty of relevant vocabulary. Think too what aspects of each topic will lead to a discussion where you have to give and justify your opinions. They're the aspects the examiner is likely to ask you about!

This section is marked on four aspects:

> ‣ **development of ideas**: a good range of relevant ideas and information, able to justify opinions

> ‣ **fluency, spontaneity and responsiveness**: responding well and with initiative, taking the lead sometimes. Of course, fluency refers to your ability to speak well on the spot, not to deliver lots of material you have learned by heart!

> ‣ **pronunciation and intonation**: sounding 'German' nearly all of the time

> ‣ **quality of language**: good use of a wide range of vocabulary and structures, and a high level of accuracy, including when using complex structures.

The material below is typical of the text you will be asked to discuss in the first part of your speaking test. Study it and write out five or six possible questions you could be asked on the content of the text, and another three more general questions related to the themes of this text. Then compare your ideas with those on page 10.

Nein zu Rassismus

Eine Erklärung der Fédération Internationale de Football Association (FIFA) gegen Rassismus und Diskriminierung wird durch die Mannschaftskapitäne in Deutschland (FIFA Confederations Cup) und in Holland (FIFA Junioren-Weltmeisterschaft) verlesen.

Am kommenden Wochenende wird vor den Viertelfinalspielen der Junior-Weltmeisterschaften in den Niederlanden und vor dem Halbfinale des Confederations Cup in Deutschland eine Erklärung der FIFA gegen Diskrminierung verlesen. Jährlich findet ein internationaler Tag des Fußball-Weltverbands statt, an dem auf Diskriminierung in diesem Sport hingewiesen und dem entgegengewirkt werden soll.

Es wird einerseits vom ‚Nein zu Rassismus‘ gesprochen, andererseits jedoch von Bekämpfung von Diskriminierung. Im Fußball wird nicht nur aufgrund von Rassismus diskriminiert, sondern – und das müsste allen Verantwortlichen bezüglich dieser Erklärung ebenfalls bekannt sein – auch aufgrund der sexuellen Orientierung. Sei es im Frauen- oder im Männerfußball: kaum jemand traut sich zu einem Outing, da dies mit existenziellen Ängsten verbunden ist. Eine Hautfarbe ist nicht zu verstecken und so sind viele Spieler nicht in der Lage, sich gegen Rassismus wehren zu können. Homosexuelle oder lesbische Fußballer/innen können hier zumindest selbst entscheiden, ob sie einen Teil ihrer Persönlichkeit geheim halten. Statistisch gesehen würde in Deutschland die Zahl schwuler Bundesligaspieler drei komplette Mannschaften der beiden Ligen stellen – also keine unerhebliche Zahl. Aufgrund der Schwulenfeindlichkeit im Fußball trauen sich einige Männer weniger in diesen Sport hinein.

:::
Use this text for practice. If possible, ask someone to put the questions for this text on page 10 to you. If not, just read them from the page and record yourself answering them. The first few questions will refer closely to the text and you should use information from it as a basis for your answers. For the more general questions, you need to be able to analyse causes, suggest solutions and give your own opinions, defending them if challenged.
:::

These are questions you might be asked about the text on page 9.

On the text itself:

▸ Was wird verlesen und von wem?

▸ Können Sie den Satz ‚Jährlich findet ein internationaler Tag des Fußball-Weltverbands statt, an dem auf Diskriminierung in diesem Sport hingewiesen und dem entgegengewirkt werden soll' erklären?

▸ Welche Diskriminierungen gibt es dem letzten Abschnitt nach beim Fußball?

▸ Warum ist man der Meinung, dass manche Männer keine Fußballspieler werden könnten?

More generally:

▸ Warum ist es Ihrer Meinung nach wichtig, gegen Feindlichkeit zu kämpfen?

▸ Sind Sie der Ansicht, dass man mit Sport gegen Rassismus kämpfen kann?

▸ Inwiefern kann man in der Schule oder in der Ausbildung gegen Diskriminierung vorgehen?

▸ Was würden Sie gegen Diskriminierung tun, wenn Sie in der Regierung wären?

For the first question, you need to find the answer in the first paragraph of the text and – this is important! – you have to express it **in your own** words. The first two sentences answer the question, but rather than read it out, you should say something like: ‚*Die Fußballkapitäne in Deutschland und Holland werden vor den Fußballspielen eine Stellungnahme gegen Fremdenfeindlichkeit und Diskriminierung vorlesen.*'

Be careful to notice that you are asked for more than one answer in the text to the question which specifies ‚*dem letzten Abschnitt nach ...* '.You need to ensure that you find both types of discrimination mentioned: racism and sexual discrimination.

For the first opinion question on the importance of combating hostility, you can use ideas from the text, for example that people are too afraid to out themselves, and that they therefore live very limited lives. But also make sure you give your own opinions. You could say something like: ‚*Es gibt viele Probleme in unserer Schule, zum Beispiel ...* ' or ‚*Wenn man in der Gesellschaft Feindlichkeit erlaubt, braucht man sich nicht zu wundern, wenn dadurch viele Probleme entstehen, zum Beispiel ...* '. Remember to have lots of well prepared ideas and examples for the range of different AS and A2 topics.

Here's another example of what the text you have to discuss might look like.

Text A – Kandidatenbogen

Sie haben 20 Minuten, um diesen Text vorzubereiten.

In der Prüfung müssen Sie:
> Fragen zum Text beantworten
> Themen, die aus dem Text entstehen, diskutieren
> Ihre Meinung zum Thema ‚Kunst und Kultur' äußern.

Kunst und Kultur

Die herrliche Landschaft und das kleinstädtische Flair zogen weltbekannte Künstler nach Murnau. Als Wassily Kandinsky und Gabriele Münter gemeinsam mit Alexej Jawlensky und Marianne Werefkin im Sommer 1908 nach Murnau kamen, entstand eine Malerei, die nicht mehr dem Vorbild der Natur im gewohnten Sinne folgte, sondern den subjektiven Eindruck erfasste und die vorangegangene ‚impressionistische' Malweise völlig hinter sich ließ. Hier schrieben die Maler des ‚Blauen Reiters' Kunstgeschichte, verfasste der Dramatiker Ödön von Horváth Theaterstücke und Romane und verschönerte der Jugendstil-Architekt Emanuel von Seidl das Ortsbild.

Traditionelle Hinterglasmalerei finden Sie in den Heimatmuseen Seehausen und Uffing sowie in der August-Ausstellung Murnauer Hinterglasmaler. Über die regionale Entwicklungsgeschichte der Hinterglasmalerei hinaus zeigt das Schloßmuseum die Vielfalt dieser Kunst im internationalen Vergleich. Das Schloßmuseum Murnau beherbergt u. a. die weltweit größte, ständige Ausstellung von Münter-Bildern und die einzige Ausstellung über den Dramatiker Ödön von Horváth mit einer Retrospektive seiner Murnauer Jahre (1923–1933).

Auch heute zeugen Ateliers und Galerien von der lebendigen Künstlerszene in Murnau.

Die enge Verbindung von Kunst und Musik in Murnau sind Zeugnis der Freundschaft zwischen Arnold Schönberg und Wassily Kandinsky. Während sich Schönberg im Malen versuchte, komponierte Kandinsky den ‚Gelben Klang'. Die Musik nimmt in Murnau einen hohen Stellenwert ein. So gibt es hier eine eigene Musikschule und mehrere Orchester, Chöre und Musikgruppen, die das Kulturprogramm des Ortes bereichern. Zu den Höhepunkten zählen die Kulturwoche, das Jazzfestival, das Musikfestival ‚grenzenlos' und der ‚KultUrknall'.

Read and listen to this student's answers to the questions at the beginning of his speaking test (CD track 2). He is discussing the text on page 11.

Weshalb ist Murnau bekannt, dem ersten Abschnitt nach zu urteilen?

Hier steht, dass Murnau bekannt ist, weil einige weltberühmte Maler und Künstler nach Murnau kamen, wo sie neue Ideen fanden. Der Architekt von Seidl hat zum Beispiel das Ortsbild verschönert und der Dramatiker von Horváth seine Meisterwerke hier geschrieben. Sie kamen, weil die Landschaft schön ist.

Über welche zwei Ausstellungen wird hier berichtet?

Die zwei Ausstellungen, über die hier berichtet wird, sind die über Hinterglasmalerei im Heimatmuseum und über die Münter-Bilder im Schloßmuseum.

Erklären Sie den Begriff im dritten Abschnitt: ‚die lebendige Künstlerszene'.

‚Die lebendige Künstlerszene' bedeutet die Gruppe der Maler, Musiker und anderen Künstler, die noch in Murnau wohnen und Kunst schaffen. Im Ort gibt es nicht nur Ausstellungen über diese bekannten Künstler, sondern auch über neue Künstler.

In welcher Weise kann man am Kulturerbe in Murnau teilhaben?

Man kann die bereits genannten Ausstellungen besuchen, wenn man sich für Kunst oder für Literatur interessiert. Man könnte auch die Musikschule besuchen oder dem Orchester, einem Chor oder einer Musikgruppe beitreten. Man kann auch Karten für das Jazzfestival oder das Musikfestival kaufen.

Inwiefern sind diese Angebote Ihrer Meinung nach für Jugendliche interessant?

Meiner Meinung nach gibt es viele interessante Angebote hier, die für viele Jugendliche in Frage kämen, weil viele Musik lieben. Ich selbst aber finde Kunst nicht sehr interessant, und ich glaube nicht, dass viele Jugendliche diese Ausstellungen interessant finden.

Wie kann man bei Jugendlichen das Interesse an Kunst wecken?

Ich glaube, Jugendliche finden Kunst uninteressant, weil es nicht sehr modern und zeitbezogen ist. Meiner Meinung nach sollte man in den Museen mehr Graffitti und darstellende Kunst sehen und dann würden auch mehr Jugendliche kommen. Ich glaube auch, dass ein Jazzfestival die Jugend nicht anspricht. Junge Leute interessieren sich doch eher für Rockmusik. Jugendliche sollten die Gelegenheit haben, selbst Festivals zu organisieren. Das wäre besser.

The examiner will move on to other opinion-based questions linked to the theme of the article, perhaps your opinions on what would be important in a successful cultural festival, the role of the arts in society, or how culture can bring countries together.

For the second part of the Speaking Test, you will be asked to discuss one of your chosen topics, i.e. a specific angle on one of the sub-topics listed on page 4. If this doesn't last the full time, the examiner will move on to your second topic. Here are a few sample questions: those marked ** are the sort of question which might be used to start the discussion, while the rest are examples of what might come up later on. Remember that the discussion should always relate to Germany or German-speaking countries. You can listen to students answering some of these questions on the CD (track 3) and find a transcript in a word document on the CD ROM.

Integration and exclusion
▶ Was sind die Hauptgründe der Diskriminierung in der deutschen Gesellschaft? **
▶ Finden Sie es richtig, dass man Neonazis und Rechtsextremismus in Deutschland nicht mehr toleriert?

Law and order
▶ Welche Aspekte der Kriminalität sind heutzutage in Deutschland wichtig? **
▶ Hat die Polizei genügend Ressourcen, um gegen Kriminalität anzugehen?
▶ Was sind die Hauptgründe der Jugendkriminalität?

Unemployment
▶ Was wissen Sie über Arbeitslosigkeit heutzutage in Deutschland? **
▶ Könnten Arbeitslose Ihrer Meinung nach immer eine Arbeit finden, wenn sie wollten?
▶ Was sind Ihrer Meinung nach die Folgen der Arbeitslosigkeit für die Gesellschaft?

The individual and the environment
▶ Wie hat man in Deutschland versucht, mehr Menschen umweltbewusster zu machen? **
▶ Was sollte man tun, um seine eigene CO_2-Bilanz zu reduzieren?
▶ Was ist das Wichtigste, das alle tun könnten, um der Umwelt zu helfen?

Energy management
▶ Wie sehen Sie die Entwicklung erneuerbarer Energien in Deutschland? **
▶ Glauben Sie, dass erneuerbare Energien eines Tages den Energiebedarf decken könnten?
▶ Wie wichtig ist Ihrer Meinung nach Atomkraft in Deutschland?

Pollution

▸ Sprechen Sie darüber, wie man in Deutschland versucht, Umweltverschmutzung zu bekämpfen. **

▸ Ist es unvermeidlich, dass man Probleme mit Umweltverschmutzung hat, wenn man in einem Industriestaat lebt?

Conservation of the natural world

▸ Spielen die Grünen noch eine wichtige Rolle in der deutschen Umweltpolitik? **

▸ Muss man sich Sorgen über das Absterben der Nordsee machen?

▸ Sollte man in der Schule mehr über Umweltschutz lernen?

Medical progress

▸ Welche medizinischen Fortschritte werden zurzeit in Deutschland besprochen? **

▸ Welche Vorteile bringt menschliches Klonen mit sich? Halten Sie es für richtig?

Scientific advances

▸ Welche wichtigen deutschen wissenschaftlichen Erfindungen kennen Sie? **

▸ Sollte man Genmanipulation in Deutschland erlauben?

▸ Wird es vielleicht in Zukunft aufgrund der Fortschritte in der Wissenschaft keine Krankheiten mehr geben?

Technological developments

▸ Inwiefern kann man sagen, dass Deutschland neue Technologien annimmt? **

▸ Welche Aspekte der neuen Technologien sehen Sie als negativ?

▸ Finden Sie es nötig, dass man für jedes Problem eine technologische Antwort haben muss?

Literature and the arts

▸ Sprechen Sie über das Werk eines Autors/einer Autorin, eines Regisseurs/einer Regisseurin oder eines Malers/einer Malerin, den Sie bewundern. **

▸ Wie werden Künstler in Deutschland besonders unterstützt? **

Political issues

▸ Welche Aspekte der deutschen politischen Struktur interessieren Sie am meisten? **

▸ Werden Sie bei den nächsten Wahlen wählen? Warum (nicht)?

▸ Glauben Sie, dass man sich in Deutschland für Europa ausspricht?

Heritage and history

▸ Welchen Aspekt der deutschen Geschichte haben Sie gewählt und warum? **

▸ Welche Vorteile gibt es, wenn alle Geschichte in der Schule lernen?

The Listening, Reading and Writing paper

You can plan your time as you wish, but it is suggested that you allocate it roughly as follows:

half an hour for Section A (Listening and Writing)
one hour for Section B (Reading and Writing)
one hour and a quarter for Section C (Writing).

Section A: Listening and Writing (35 marks), including 5 marks for Quality of Language

You will be able to play, replay and pause the recordings yourself. There will be two passages to listen to:

▶ one with questions in English
▶ one with questions in German.

Section B: Reading and Writing (60 marks), including 5 marks for Quality of Language

There will be two different passages of German to read, each with a variety of types of exercise.

After reading the first passage, you will be asked to do the following:

▶ a non-verbal task, such as multiple choice, ticking the correct statements, choosing appropriate expressions to match words or phrases from the text or finding synonyms
▶ an exercise where you have to manipulate language, such as gap-filling or completing sentences
▶ answer questions in German
▶ explain words underlined in the text.

After reading the second passage, you will be asked to do the following:

▶ transfer of language into English
▶ two tasks requiring language manipulation, such as completing sentences, filling gaps and answering questions in German.

Section C: Writing (45 marks)

You have to write one essay IN GERMAN of at least 250 words and the suggested maximum is 400 words. There will be two questions on each of the four main topics from the specification: *Die Gesellschaft, Die Umwelt, Wissenschaft und Technologie* and *Kultur*.

> The key ways to prepare are by:
>
> ▶ doing plenty of listening practice to keep your ear 'tuned in' to German
> ▶ reading a wide variety of materials linked to the topics listed on page 4
> ▶ practising writing essays on the topics you have studied – allow yourself an hour and write between 250 and 400 words.
> ▶ working through the exam-type questions and tips on the following pages.

Rache   CD track 4

Listen to the report, then answer the following questions IN ENGLISH.

a What was reported to have happened at the dog school? (2)
b What developments have there been in the last few days? (2)
c What did Günther Ruckdäschel declare he had found out? (2)
d Did the police manage to question all the policewomen? (1)
e Do they know the identity of the sender? (1)
f What punishment is going to befall the letter's sender? (2)

Be especially careful over questions with more than one mark and be
sure you give all the relevant detail. When you have done this exercise,
read the answer section carefully and take note of how the marks were
allocated for questions a, b, c and f.

a That there was sexual abuse of policewomen (1) and inhumane treatment of
dogs (1).
b The allegations have been proven to be false (1) and there has been a
sensational turnaround (1).
c All the witnesses declared that they weren't sexually abused (1) nor were they
insulted (1).
d No, 15 out of the 16.
e He is still unknown.
f He will be prosecuted for false accusation (1) and slander (1).

Die in den letzten Tagen als Skandal offengelegten sexistischen Misshandlungen
von Polizistinnen und der menschenunwürdige Umgang an der bayrischen
Polizeihundeschule haben sich als falsch erwiesen. Damit gab es in dem Fall, der
in den letzten Tagen für erhebliches Aufsehen in Deutschland gesorgt hat, eine
geradezu sensationelle Wende.

Die Ermittlungen der Staatsanwaltschaft und die durchgeführten Befragungen
von Zeuginnen haben keine Bestätigungen für die Anschuldigungen in einem
anonymen Brief ergeben. Der Leiter der Oberstaatsanwaltschaft, Günther
Ruckdäschel, teilte mit, dass alle Zeuginnen erklärt haben, „sie seien in Herzogau
niemals zu irgendwelchen Handlungen gezwungen oder auch beleidigt worden".

Die Staatsanwaltschaft hat 15 der 16 in den letzten drei Jahren in
Herzogau ausgebildeten Polizistinnen befragt. Dabei haben sich keinerlei
Anhaltspunkte ergeben, die die Anschuldigungen bestätigen würden.
Auch an der Glaubwürdigkeit der Beamtinnen bestehe kein Zweifel, so die
Staatsanwaltschaft.

Es wird jetzt vermutet, dass es sich bei dem anonymen Brief, durch den die
Ermittlungen ins Rollen kamen, um einen Racheakt handelt. Da der Absender
des Briefes nach wie vor unbekannt ist, wird es zu einer Anklage wegen
Verleumdung und falscher Verdächtigung gegen Unbekannt kommen.

In einer Sekunde mit der Kreditkarte zahlen   CD track 5

Hören Sie sich diesen Bericht über schnelles Zahlen mit Kreditkarten an und beantworten Sie die folgenden Fragen AUF DEUTSCH.

a Was kann man mit der neuen Technologie machen? (3)
b Wie lange dauert dieser Vorgang? (1)
c Erklären Sie, was man in Singapur schon machen kann. (2)
d Was muss man in Deutschland machen? (1)
e Welche drei Vorteile erwähnen die Unternehmen? (3)

> Make sure you know exactly what every question form means. The ones here are *was* - what, *wie lange* - how long, and *welche* - which. Other common question forms are *wer* (who), *warum* (why), *wo* (where) and *wie viel* (how much/many). If you are asked to explain 'why', don't tell the examiner 'when'!

a Man kann Minibeträge bequemer begleichen (1), bis zu 25 Euro (1) mit einer Kreditkarte (1).
b eine Sekunde (1)
c an der U-Bahn zahlen (1); beim Einkauf zahlen (1)
d nach seinem Kleingeld suchen (1)
e Es ist einfach (1), bequem (1) und zeitsparend (1).

Künftig können die Deutschen Minibeträge bequemer begleichen. Mit einer neuen Technologie können Besitzer von Kreditkarten Summen bis zu 25 Euro durch Vorbeiziehen der Karte an einem Lesegerät zahlen. Der Zahlvorgang ist in einer Sekunde erledigt.

Wer schon einmal in Hongkong, Singapur oder Schanghai war, wird es verwundert beobachtet haben. In der U-Bahn halten die Menschen einfach nur ihren Geldbeutel an ein Lesegerät und die Zugangsschranke öffnet sich. Oder am Kiosk: Portemonnaie an den kleinen Terminal an der Kasse halten und der Einkauf ist bezahlt. Das Gleiche gilt im Taxi, beim Bäcker, beim Burger-Brater.

Hierzulande suchen Menschen bei solchen Gelegenheiten nach wie vor mühsam ihr Kleingeld zusammen. Doch es gibt Hoffnung, dass dies bald ein Ende hat. Denn die Kreditkartenunternehmen wollen auch den Deutschen beibringen, wie man Kleinbeträge einfach, bequem und vor allem zeitsparend bezahlen kann. Wird die Kreditkarte mit dieser Technologie ausgestattet, so soll der Besitzer damit künftig Beträge bis zu 25 Euro durch ein einfaches kurzes Vorbeiführen der Karte an einem Lesegerät begleichen können. Weder das Eingeben einer Pin-Nummer noch eine Unterschrift sind nötig.

Lesen Sie den Bericht über Rassismus in Deutschland und beantworten Sie die Fragen AUF DEUTSCH.

Rassismus in Deutschland

1 Die Vereinten Nationen sind besorgt über eine zunehmende Zahl rassistischer Vorfälle in Deutschland. Betroffen seien vor allem Juden, Moslems, Sinti und Roma sowie afrikanische Asylbewerber, heißt es in einem am Freitag in Genf verabschiedeten Bericht des UN-Ausschusses zur Beseitigung rassistischer Diskriminierung (CERD).

2 Das Bundesjustizministerium will die Empfehlungen des Ausschusses prüfen und sorgfältig auswerten. Für eine Stellungnahme sei es noch zu früh, sagte ein Sprecher. Der Ausschuss kritisierte, dass im deutschen Strafrecht die rassistische Motivation von Verbrechen nicht ausdrücklich als strafverschärfend angesehen werde. Nach Angaben des UN-Gremiums bekommen zudem Ausländer, die Opfer von Gewalttaten wurden, nach dem Opferentschädigungsgesetz meist weniger Geld zugesprochen als Deutsche.

3 Die Internationale Liga für Menschenrechte erklärte, der Ausschuss habe „in ungewöhnlich deutlicher Form" die Missstände in Deutschland benannt. Es sei klar geworden, dass die Bundesregierung nicht entschieden genug gegen Rassismus vorgehe.

4 Insbesondere ging der UN-Ausschuss in seinem Bericht auf die Situation der Sinti und Roma ein. Sie würden unter anderem bei der Bildung sowie auf dem Arbeits- und Wohnungsmarkt benachteiligt, hieß es. Auch in den Medien werde diese Volksgruppe häufig diskriminiert.

1 Welche Gruppen werden dem Bericht der UN nach diskriminiert? (3)

2 Was sagte der Sprecher des Bundesjustizmimisteriums über eine Stellungnahme? (1)

3 Wie hat die UN Deutschland in Bezug auf finanzielle Unterstützung kritisiert? (3)

4 Inwiefern sieht der UN-Ausschuss die Sinti und Roma benachteiligt? (3)

> You can often use ideas and short phrases from the text, but you should not be copying whole sentences from it and will usually have to adapt the language. For question 2, the part about the report is in the **subjunctive** because it is reported speech. You can use the subjunctive for your answer, or you can use *Er sagte, dass …* and use the present tense. For all the questions, try to think of synonyms for the expressions you need to use. Look at the answers for some ideas.

1 Three of: Der UN nach sind Juden (1), Moslems (1), Sinti (1), Roma (1) und afrikanische Asylbewerber (1) von Diskriminierung betroffen.

2 Er sagte, es sei zu früh für eine Stellungnahme. (1)

3 In Deutschland werden Straftaten gegen Ausländer nicht hart genug bestraft (1), und außerdem bekommen sie weniger Geld (1) als Entschädigung, wenn sie Opfer einer Gewalttat werden. (1)

4 Three of: Sinti und Roma werden in der Schule (1), bei der Arbeit (1), bei der Wohnungssuche (1) und in den Medien (1) diskriminierend behandelt.

Erklären Sie AUF DEUTSCH die folgenden im Text unterstrichenen Ausdrücke.

Tanzen gegen Gewalt

Wir, der Verein Lichtblick E.V., haben eine Party Night als eine Benefiz-Veranstaltung für Opfer von Missbrauch, Gewalt und Rassismus ins Leben gerufen. Wir haben uns gedacht, dass es doch Möglichkeiten geben muss, <u>Zeichen</u> gegen Gewalt zu setzen. Warum dann nicht bei einer Veranstaltung, wo gesungen, getanzt und gelacht wird? Warum nicht gemeinsam gegen Gewalt tanzen?

Den kompletten <u>Erlös</u> aus der Party Night spenden wir für ein Projekt gegen Gewalt. In unserem Startjahr 2007 haben wir den Erlös Projekten wie ‚Buddy-Kids‘ und ‚Teen-Defence‘ zukommen lassen. Es werden in jedem Jahr neue und andere Projekte unterstützt. Welche das sind, erfahren Sie in unseren Ankündigungen zur <u>jeweiligen</u> Party. Falls Sie eine Organisation kennen, die es auch mal ‚verdient‘ hat, unterstützt zu werden, scheuen Sie sich nicht und nehmen Sie Kontakt mit uns auf.

Die Party Night organisieren wir immer für Anfang September. Den jeweiligen genauen Termin können Sie ebenfalls unseren Ankündigungen entnehmen.

Aufgabe 1

Hier sind einige Wörter aus dem Text. Haken Sie die richtige Bedeutung für jedes Wort an. Die Wörter sind unterstrichen.

a Zeichen
    i malen ☐
    ii es sieht so aus ☐
    iii Hinweis ☐

b Erlös
    i Männer ☐
    ii Gelder ☐
    iii Karten ☐

c jeweiligen
    i entsprechenden ☐
    ii jemanden ☐
    iii jeden ☐

Collecting pairs of synonyms is an excellent way to enlarge your vocabulary and it is especially useful in preparation for exercises such as this. Start a section in your vocabulary notes for synonyms and note them down as you find them in exercises or as they occur to you when reading. As a start, copy down these words and give a synonym for each: *schnell, leicht, Bericht, hassen, Probleme, Zukunft.*

The Listening, Reading and Writing paper

Aufgabe 2

Füllen Sie die Lücken in dieser Zusammenfassung des Textes aus, um zu zeigen, dass Sie alles verstanden haben. Sie dürfen die Wörter dem Text entnehmen, wenn sie passen.

Lichtblick haben eine Party, die jedes Jahr im September **(a)**_____, organisiert, um Opfer der Gewalt zu helfen, denn sie wollen Zeichen gegen Gewalt **(b)**_____ und gemeinsam durch Tanzen Gewalt **(c)**_____. Das **(d)**_____ Geld wird gespendet, und jedes Jahr wird ein **(e)**_____ Projekt unterstützt. Falls Sie mehr Information haben wollen, **(f)**_____ Sie sie aus deren Infomationen entnehmen.

> You really need to understand both texts well to do this kind of activity. You need to find a word for each gap which fits grammatically and keeps the sense of the original passage. Sometimes you can use a word from the original text – gap **b** is a good example because you could use *setzen*. But more often, you need to adapt a word. For gap **a** you need a verb and you need to make sure you check what it is referring to. For gap **c**, you need to ensure you remember to use the infinitive following the verb *wollen*.

Aufgabe 3

Finden Sie die Wörter, die genau mit den folgenden Ausdrücken übereinstimmen.

a Ereignis
b zuteil werden
c herausfinden
d kennen

> Sometimes the expressions match exactly grammatically, as in question **a** where you need to find a noun in the text with the same meaning. But you only need one word for the two-word expression in question **b**.

The Listening, Reading and Writing paper

This exercise is good practice but in fact the exam task will be easier in two ways: the passage will be shorter (about 50 words) and it will be part of a text to be worked on for the other reading activities.

Translate the following passage INTO ENGLISH.

Um die Säugetiere der Erde steht es nicht gut: Zwischen 25 und 36 Prozent sind vom Aussterben bedroht. Zu diesem Ergebnis kam eine Kommission von über 1800 Wissenschaftlern aus 130 Ländern unter der Leitung der International Union for Conservation of Nature (IUCN). Verantwortlich für den Artenschwund sind unter anderem der Verlust von Lebensräumen, die Umweltverschmutzung und die Jagd auf bedrohte Tierarten. Die Studie zeigt zum ersten Mal umfassend den Zustand der Land- und Meeressäugetiere auf der ganzen Erde auf.

Remember that German word order can at times be very different from English word order. You need to be careful as well that you don't translate items literally but think about their meaning.

Remember that a literal translation will not always sound right in English. What expression would be better than 'stands not good' for 'steht es nicht gut'? What word will you use to translate 'Artenschwund'?

Where possible, keep your English translation closely in line with the German because doing so cuts down the risk of missing out parts of the sentence. But there are some marks for Quality of Language and sometimes the English version will sound more natural if you alter the word order. This has been done below: compare the two versions carefully.

The mammals on Earth are not in a good place: between 25 and 36 percent are threatened by extinction. This is the conclusion arrived at by a commission made up of over 1,800 scientists from 130 countries under the leadership of the International Union for Conservation of Nature (IUCN). Loss of habitat, pollution and hunting of endangered species are, among other things, responsible for the dwindling of the species. The study shows broadly for the first time the global state of land and sea mammals.

Lesen Sie den Text und schreiben Sie die folgenden Sätze zu Ende. Sie können den Satz jeweils mit einem oder mit mehreren Wörtern beenden.

Brot für die Welt

1 Im bitteren Widerspruch zu dem Versprechen der Vereinten Nationen, die Anzahl der Hungernden bis 2015 zu halbieren, steigt der Hunger weltweit weiter an. Grund dafür ist der rasante Anstieg der Preise für Grundnahrungsmittel. Allein in der ersten Hälfte des Jahres 2008 hat sich der Preis von Reis, Mais und Weizen nahezu verdoppelt. Dadurch reichte das Einkommen vieler armer Menschen nicht mehr aus, um Grundnahrungsmittel zu kaufen.

2 Ohne genügend Geld für Hilfsprogramme drohten „weit verbreiteter Hunger, Mangelernährung und soziale Unruhen in noch nie da gewesenem Ausmaß", warnte UN-Generalsekretär Ban Ki Moon nach Beratungen von 27 UN-Institutionen über die hohen Nahrungsmittelpreise im April 2008. Ban setzte eine internationale Arbeitsgruppe ein, die Sofortmaßnahmen koordinieren und längerfristige Strategien zur Hungerbekämpfung entwerfen solle.

3 „Die derzeitige Krise bietet die Chance, die Weichen für eine verantwortliche Politik im Bereich Landwirtschaft und Agrarhandel zu stellen", betont Cornelia Füllkrug-Weitzel, Direktorin von ‚Brot für die Welt', und fordert die Bundesregierung auf, in Europa eine Führungsrolle bei der weltweiten Hungerbekämpfung zu übernehmen.

a (1) Die Vereinten Nationen haben sich vorgenommen, die Anzahl der ...
b (1) Aber die Anzahl der Hungernden ...
c (1) Der Grund dafür ist der schnelle ...
d (1) Das Einkommen vieler Menschen ...
e (2) Ban hat eine Arbeitsgruppe eingesetzt, um ...
f (3) Füllkrug-Weitzel möchte, dass Deutschland eine Führungsrolle bei der Hungerbekämpfung ...

Make sure you continue the sentence in a way which fits grammatically. Remember that after the conjunction *die* the verb is sent to the end, as in **a**. In **d**, remember to use the imperfect tense, like in the text. In **e**, remember you need to add an infinitive with *zu* after *um*. In **b** and **f**, remember to use the verb in the correct form – here, third person singular.

f übernimmt.

e die Sofortmaßnahmen zu koordinieren / längerfristige Strategien zur Hungerbekämpfung zu entwerfen.

d reichte nicht mehr aus.

c Anstieg der Preise für Grundnahrungsmittel.

b steigt weiter an.

a Hungernden in der Welt bis 2015 zu halbieren.

The Listening, Reading and Writing paper

Lesen Sie den Text und erklären Sie AUF DEUTSCH die folgenden im Text unterstrichenen Ausdrücke.

Zwischen Arm und Reich

Der neue Armuts- und Reichtumsbericht der Bundesregierung hat den Streit um die soziale Kluft in Deutschland <u>nochmals</u> angeheizt. Dem Bericht <u>zufolge</u> ist inzwischen jeder vierte Deutsche arm oder muss durch staatliche Leistungen vor Armut <u>bewahrt</u> werden. 13 Prozent der Bundesbürger gelten laut des Berichts als arm; weitere 13 Prozent würden durch Sozialhilfen wie Kindergeld oder Arbeitslosengeld vor dem <u>Abrutschen</u> in Armut bewahrt, so Bundesarbeitsminister Olaf Scholz (SPD). Im Gegenzug seien die Einkünfte der Reichen weiter <u>gewachsen</u>. „Die Schere zwischen Arm und Reich hat sich weiter geöffnet", so Scholz. „Arm ist laut EU-Definition, wer als Alleinlebender weniger als 60 Prozent des mittleren <u>Einkommens</u> verdient, also 781 Euro netto", sagte Scholz. Als reich gelte, wer als Alleinlebender im Monat netto mehr als 3418 Euro zur Verfügung habe oder als Familie mit zwei Kindern mehr als 7178 Euro netto im Monat. FDP-Generalsekretär Dirk Niebel warf Scholz vor, er beklage die <u>Auswirkungen</u> einer Politik, „die er und seine SPD zu verantworten haben". Die FDP hatte die Agenda-Politik in der Vergangenheit immer wieder gelobt und mit vorangetrieben.

a nochmals
b zufolge
c bewahrt
d Abrutschen
e gewachsen
f Einkommens
g Auswirkungen

> Be careful to look at each word or phrase in its context in the passage before you decide on a possible alternative. Read the sentence of the passage to yourself with your suggested phrase in it and make sure it fits grammatically and keeps the sense of the original version.

> Think creatively! The suggested answers for sentences **d**, **f** and **g** must be nouns, but make sure you also check the case and whether it needs to be singular or plural. Remember that the answers to **c** and **e** must be in the perfect tense.

a wieder   b nach   c geschont   d Fall   e gestiegen
f Verdienstes   g Folgen

Writing an Essay on a Cultural Topic

You have to write one essay on one of the topics you have studied (see page 4 for a full list). You must write a minimum of 250 words and the suggested maximum is 400. The three vital stages are planning, writing and checking.

Planning

Don't rush this stage. 5–10 minutes thinking about the question, deciding on your argument and dividing it into paragraphs, jotting down the facts you want to use and thinking out a good introduction and conclusion is time very well spent. Keep referring to the title to make sure every paragraph is relevant to the question. Make sure you use information relating to Germany or a German-speaking country to illustrate and support your argument. You might also note vocabulary and phrases you want to use in each paragraph. Then, when everything is in order, start writing, and make sure you stick to the plan!

Writing

Work through your notes for each paragraph. Write them up using a variety of sentence lengths, interesting vocabulary and a range of grammatical constructions. Be especially careful about the links between the paragraphs, so the examiner can follow the argument easily. A phrase like *'Man muss sagen / dazu behaupten ...'* can introduce ideas which build on those in the previous paragraph, but if you want to move on to a different angle you might start with *'Auf der anderen Seite ...'* or *'Jedoch muss man auch sagen, dass ...'*

Checking

Read your essay once through to check the flow of ideas and make sure each sentence makes sense. Then do a more detailed check, looking especially for these common errors:

▶ verbs which don't agree with their subject or are in the wrong tense
▶ adjectives which don't match the noun they describe
▶ phrases which are not idiomatic and don't sound German
▶ misspellings, especially of words similar to, but not the same as, English
▶ missing umlauts and capital letters
▶ word order: time – manner – place phrases, verbs in the correct place, past participles at the end of the sentence.

The marks for this question are awarded as follows:

▶ **structure and analysis**: 15 marks, i.e. a well structured, logical argument which shows you can analyse, evaluate and draw conclusions.
▶ **relevance and points of view**: 10 marks, i.e. views and opinions which are relevant to the question and are well supported by a good use of information.
▶ **range of language**: 10 marks, i.e. showing a wide vocabulary and a good range of complex structures.
▶ **accuracy**: 10 marks, i.e. a high level of accuracy throughout, including when using complex structures, although there may be a few errors.

All the grammar you learned for AS is still needed, and there are some extra points for A2. Pages 26–32 revise AS grammar, reminding you what you should know and giving you phrases and sentences to translate from and into German for practice. Pages 33–34 revise the points you will be learning on the A2 course, also practised through sentences to translate.

Grammar is even more important at A2 than it was at AS. So, what can you to do make sure you really do know your stuff?

Pay attention when grammar is explained. If you learn the rules and the exceptions and do some practice exercises, you will be surprised how much of it will stick.

Accept that there is quite a lot of detail to master and be prepared to go over things regularly. Re-read your grammar notes, re-do practice exercises, ask questions if you come across things you don't fully understand.

Be pro-active. Go through marked written work, looking carefully at the things which have been corrected. Decide which ones are 'silly mistakes', caused by forgetting things which you know well and make a list of them, so you can try to avoid them in future. Then look for errors where you are not quite sure why it is wrong. Ask, if necessary, then look up that grammar point in the grammar section of your textbook and in the relevant section of the grammar workbook. Keep practising and asking questions until you do understand it. When you understand it, review it by writing grammar notes on it in your own words, adding examples.

Make a list of example sentences from your written work which use some of the more complex grammar points well. Learn them, and use them as models for other sentences with different vocabulary but which use the same basic structure. Make a point of including a good variety of grammatical structures in the practice essays you write.

Work through the exercises on the following pages. If there are practice sentences you find hard to translate, learn the correct version from the answer section by heart.

Revision of AS Grammar: nouns, adjectives, adverbs

Check the grammar section of *Zeitgeist 2* and/or the Grammar Workbook if you need to know more about any of these things:

▸ typical masculine endings for nouns, such as *-ant, -er, -ich, -ig, -ing, -ismus,* etc

▸ typical feminine endings for nouns, such as *-e, -heit, -ik, -ın, keit, -schaft, -ung,* etc

▸ typical neuter endings for nouns, such as *-chen, -lein, -um,* etc

▸ how to form the plurals of nouns – is it *-n, -en, -nen, -s, -er* and does it have an umlaut? Or does it require a plural at all?

▸ how to make adjectives agree in number and case

▸ forming possessive adjectives like *mein, dein, sein, ihr, unser,* etc

▸ using *kein* with appropriate endings to translate the negative

▸ using adjectives as adverbs

▸ comparing adjectives by adding *-er* plus the appropriate adjective ending

▸ using the superlative by adding *-(e)st* to the adjective as well as the appropriate ending and not forgetting the definite article *der, die* or *das*

▸ using irregular comparisons like *besser* and *höher* or irregular superlatives like *(das) beste* and *(das) nächste.*

(1) Translate into English:

1 Man muss kälteres Wasser in der Waschmaschine benutzen.
2 Die Ausbeutung der Wälder zeigt keinen Respekt für die Natur.
3 Das nächste Mal erwarten wir etwas Besseres!
4 Kohlenstoff hat die schlimmste Auswirkung auf unserer Atmosphäre.
5 Wir haben keine realistischeren Lösungen.
6 Was muss man machen, um den richtigen Weg zu finden?
7 Die Transportsysteme der Zukunft werden viel effizienter sein.
8 Eine reichhaltige Diät ist besser für die Gesundheit.
9 Klar bin ich viel optimistischer als du!
10 Die Sonne ist eine direkte Quelle von Licht und Wärme.

Translate into German:

11 Trains are more environmentally friendly than cars.
12 We have enough gas, but no petrol.
13 An old car is not good for the environment.
14 A new car is just as bad as an old one.
15 Their house has solar panels.
16 My central heating is expensive.
17 There's a good atmosphere in the eco-village.
18 People there live more cheaply than we do.
19 Do you recycle old newspapers and empty bottles?
20 Which energy is the cheapest?

Revision of AS Grammar: pronouns

Check the grammar section of *Zeitgeist 2* and/or the Grammar Workbook if you need to know more about any of these things:
- direct object pronouns: *mich, dich, sich, uns, euch, ihnen*
- indirect object pronouns: *mir, dir, sich*
- reflexive pronouns used with reflexive verbs: *mich, dich, sich, uns, euch*
- the relative pronouns *der, die, das,dessen, deren*
- indefinite pronouns *jemand, niemand, jeder.*

(2) Translate into English:

1 Immigranten? Bezahlt man ihnen Kindergeld?
2 Laut des deutschen Grundgesetzes darf niemand wegen seiner Rasse benachteiligt werden.
3 Immigranten sind mit ihren Familien nach Deutschland gekommen.
4 In den letzten hundert Jahren haben deutsche Aussiedler wegen ihrer Nationalität viel gelitten.
5 Jeder hat das Recht auf die Nationalität vom Land seiner Geburt.
6 Immigranten sind zum Arbeiten in unser Land gekommen.
7 Wir sind gegen jeden, der die Menschenrechte nicht respektiert.
8 Deutschland ist das Land, in dem ich aufgewachsen bin und dessen Kultur ich mich anzupassen versuche.
9 Man erlaubt mir nicht, meine Herkunft zu vergessen.
10 Man wird nirgendwo als zugehörig betrachtet.

Translate into German:
11 Explain racism to me.
12 I told them I do not understand them.
13 He lives in Leipzig now and finds it very peaceful.
14 It is a town that I don't know.
15 Guest workers are mainly Turks, who came to Germany for work.
16 The resettlers are Germans who now live in Eastern Europe.
17 They have lived there for 20 years.
18 The map? Show me it, please.
19 Xenophobia – what is the cause?
20 We must try to replace it with tolerance.

Revision of AS Grammar: infinitives and the present tense

Check the grammar section of *Zeitgeist 2* and/or the Grammar Workbook if you need to know more about any of these things:

▶ the use of the infinitive construction with *zu*

▶ the use of modal verbs plus the infinitive

▶ the infinitive with *um ... zu*

▶ the present tense of regular verbs such as *wohnen, leben, arbeiten*

▶ the present tense of the modal verbs *wollen, sollen, dürfen, mögen, müssen, können*

▶ the present tense of irregular verbs such as *gehen, fahren, haben, sein, werden*

▶ the use of the present tense with *seit*

▶ the use of some verbs which take the dative such as *helfen, geben*.

(3) Translate into English:

1 Wie sind diese Probleme zu lösen?
2 Machen Sie schon etwas, um Geld für eine Wohlfahrtsorganisation aufzubringen?
3 Was brauchen solche Wohlfahrtsorganisationen, um funktionieren zu können?
4 Wir müssen eine langfristige Lösung finden.
5 Ohne Job kann man die Miete nicht bezahlen.
6 Ohne Unterkunft ist es schwierig, einen Job zu finden.
7 Wir versuchen, diesen Leuten zu helfen, ihre Gesellschaft wieder aufzubauen.
8 Den Entwicklungsländern sollte erlaubt sein, ihre Schulden bei den Industrieländern zu vergessen.
9 Wir dürfen nicht vergessen, dass alle Menschen Hilfe brauchen.
10 Wenn man in absoluter Armut lebt, hat man nicht genug zu essen.

Translate into German:
11 Everyone should have a certain standard of living.
12 Do you work for a charity?
13 I want to help people to have a future.
14 In many countries, lots of people cannot write or read.
15 I hope to be able to help them.
16 She wants to go to Africa to help the children there.
17 We have been working there for ten years.
18 Life can be very difficult for single mothers.
19 Lots of young people want to be rich.
20 What do you do if you can't find a job?

Revision of AS Grammar: past tenses

Check the grammar section of *Zeitgeist 2* and/or the Grammar Workbook if you need to know more about any of these things:
- the perfect tense with *haben: ich habe ... gemacht, ich habe ... gespielt*
- the perfect tense with *sein: ich bin ... gegangen, ich bin ... gefahren*
- the perfect tense of irregular verbs: *ich habe gesehen, ich habe gegessen*
- the perfect tense of separable verbs: *ich bin ... abgefahren, ich habe ... festgestellt*
- the imperfect tense: *er stand, ich sah, wir gingen*
- the pluperfect tense: *er hatte ... gesehen, ich war ... gegangen*
- the perfect tense of the passive voice: *es wurde verkauft.*

(4) Translate into English:

1 Der Dichter Johann Wolfgang von Goethe wurde 1749 geboren.
2 Karl Wilhelm Gropius hat eine Ausbildung als Landschaftsmaler in Berlin gemacht.
3 In dieser Zeit wurde die Gesellschaft von Männern beherrscht.
4 Fassbinder wurde 1945 geboren und verbrachte seine Kindheit in einem chaotischen Nachkriegsdeutschland
5 Marlene Dietrich ist in Berlin und Dessau zur Schule gegangen.
6 Im April 1930 hat sie Deutschland verlassen und ist nach Amerika ausgewandert.
7 Roland Emmerich begann seine Karriere als Regisseur in Deutschland.
8 Später hat er Ruhm in Amerika gefunden.
9 Der erste erfolgreiche Film von Wim Wenders war ‚Paris, Texas‘ (1984).
10 Sein Film ‚Der Himmel über Berlin‘ (1987) hat den Film ‚Stadt der Engel‘ (1998) mit Meg Ryan und Nicholas Cage inspiriert.

Translate into German:
11 How many people visited the Pergamon Museum in 2007?
12 This painting was sold for $78,000,000 last year.
13 Christa Wolf was born in 1929.
14 She did not believe in the dismantling of the GDR state.
15 At first, Lessing studied medicine and theology in Leipizig.
16 Later, he lived as a writer in Berlin, where he wrote for several newspapers.
17 In 1995, Franka Potente won the Bavarian Film Prize for Young Talent.
18 Tom Tykwer wrote the role of Lola in the film "Run, Lola, Run" for her.
19 Franka Potente has also written a screenplay.
20 Annette von Droste-Hülshoff wrote beautiful ballads and poems about Westphalia.

Grammar

Revision of AS Grammar: future and conditional

Check the grammar section of *Zeitgeist 2* and/or the Grammar Workbook if you need to know more about any of these things:
- using the present tense to refer to things which are going to happen soon, with mention of a future time: *Morgen gehe ich ins Kino, nächste Woche bleiben wir hier.*
- using *werden* + infinitive to refer to precise future plans: *ich werde ... wohnen, wir werden ... sehen*
- using *ich möchte* + infinitive to describe something that you would like to happen: *ich möchte ... arbeiten*
- forming the conditional tense using imperfect subjunctive of *werden* + infinitive to say what would happen in certain circumstances: *wir würden ... verbringen*
- using *wenn* with the conditional/imperfect subjunctive. (NB: unlike English, the same tense must be used in both parts of the sentence)
- forming the imperfect subjunctive: *ich wäre, ich hätte, ich ginge, ich käme.*

(5) Translate into English:

1 Morgen werden wir in einer Welt voller Computer leben.
2 In der Zukunft werden Computer Ihnen helfen, alles zu erledigen.
3 Es wird nicht mehr nötig sein, aus dem Hause zu gehen, weil man zu Hause alles haben wird, was man braucht.
4 Die Entscheidungen der Wissenschaftler werden ernste Folgen haben.
5 Aufgrund der Gentechnik wird es möglich sein, viele Erbkrankheiten zu heilen.
6 Aber in den nächsten fünf Jahren wird es keine Wunderheilmittel geben.
7 Das Manipulieren von menschlichem Erbgut könnte eine Welt voller perfekter Menschen schaffen.
8 Alle Lebensmittel werden gentechnisch verändert werden.
9 Gentechnisch veränderte Lebensmittel könnten neue Allergien verursachen.
10 Wenn man wüsste, dass solche Lebensmittel unschädlich wären, könnte man damit die Ernährungsprobleme in den Entwicklungsländern lösen.

Translate into German:

11 How will we live in the future?
12 There will be computers everywhere.
13 We will do our shopping on the Internet.
14 You'll be able to spend your holiday on the moon.
15 What will daily life be like?
16 My computer will help me make decisions.
17 Scientists will have to be very responsible.
18 I would not like to live in a perfect world.
19 People should know more about technology.
20 If I were young, I would study I.T.

Revision of AS Grammar: negatives

Check the grammar section of *Zeitgeist 2* and/or the Grammar Workbook if you need to know more about any of these things:

▸ using *nicht and nie* to negate a verb, remembering to place it near the end of the sentence

▸ using *nicht* to precede words for emphasis

▸ using indefinite pronouns: *nirgendwo, niemand*

▸ using *kein* as a negative with nouns: *keine Ahnung*

▸ using *weder ... noch* to give two balanced negatives

▸ using *nicht nur ... sondern auch* to translate 'not only ... but also'

▸ using *nichts.*

(6) Translate into English:

1 Wir dürfen nicht vergessen, dass die kulturelle Vielfalt in Europa sehr wichtig ist.
2 Haben Sie keine Angst vor der EU!
3 Im Moment hat die EU weder einen Präsidenten noch Soldaten.
4 Wir waren noch nie in Frankreich.
5 Ich habe keine Angst, meine Identität zu verlieren.
6 Alte Menschen werden nicht mehr isoliert, sondern respektiert und geschätzt sein.
7 Die EU hat nicht nur für die Zukunft gute Ideen, sondern auch konkrete Vorschläge, wie man diese Ideen finanzieren kann.
8 Europa hat nichts zu verbergen.
9 Nicht alle EU-Mitglieder wollen den Euro.
10 Die globale Wirtschaft hat kein Vertrauen in die europäischen Politiker.

Translate into German:

11 Isn't Poland a member of the EU?
12 He had not voted.
13 You will never visit Russia.
14 The EU is no longer small.
15 I would not like to be the EU President!
16 I no longer have a passport.
17 Nothing is more certain.
18 I have not a single euro left.
19 I prefer not to take my holidays in Europe.
20 I have neither the time nor the money.

Grammar

Revision of AS Grammar: word order

Word order is very important in German. You must remember the rules:
- the main verb is always the second idea
- the order of adverbs is time – manner – place
- conjunctions can change the word order: *weil, wenn* and *dass* send the verb to the end of the clause
- if a sentence begins with a subordinate clause, the subject and verb in the main clause invert to form "a verb sandwich"
- in relative clauses, the verb goes to the end of the clause (NB: relative pronouns must be used in German).

(7) Translate into English:

1 Natürlich hat sie sich sehr gefreut, als sie gute Noten bekommen hat.
2 Viele Frauen entscheiden sich für Teilzeitarbeit, wenn sie Kinder haben.
3 Er hat nicht viel in der Schule gearbeitet, aber jetzt arbeitet er fleißig in der Lehre.
4 Sie studiert in Deutschland, weil sie sehr gut Deutsch sprechen kann.
5 Da sie in einer Bank arbeiten will, hofft sie, Mathe an der Universität zu studieren.
6 Marlene Dietrich ist nach Amerika ausgewandert, weil sie die Nazis hasste.
7 ‚Lola rennt' ist die Geschichte einer Frau, die ihren Freund retten will.
8 Berlin ist eine schöne Stadt mit viel Geschichte.
9 Da man in der Schweiz verschiedene Sprachen spricht, ist es ein kompliziertes Land.
10 Brandenburg ist eines der neuen Bundesländer, die früher ein Teil der DDR waren.

Translate into German:

11 Last year, I studied at Bremen University.
12 Many young people speak foreign languages very well and therefore can find work anywhere in the EU.
13 She was not interested in big films but wanted to tell unusual stories.
14 Anne Frank liked it very much when people visited her.
15 The Stasi time was very difficult because you distrusted everyone.
16 The Nazi time was just as bad, as everyone was afraid.
17 As West Berliners could no longer go to East Berlin, many people could not go to work.
18 The wall was built because many East Germans wanted to leave the country.
19 West Berlin was very isolated because there was only one road in.
20 Marlene Dietrich was born in Berlin in 1901.

A2 Grammar: the subjunctive

What you need to know

As well as an alternative to the conditional, the subjunctive in German is used for direct or reported speech. The present and perfect subjunctive are the most useful here:

To form the present subjunctive, add the following endings to the stem of the verb:

ich -e, du -est, er/sie -e, wir -en, ihr -et, sie -en.

The exception to this is *sein:*

ich sei, du seiest, er sei, wir seien, ihr seiet, sie seien.

The perfect subjunctive is formed quite logically with the present subjunctive of the auxiliary *haben* or *sein* plus the past participle: *ich sei gegangen, ich habe gemacht.*

The imperfect subjunctive is often used for politeness, expressing wishes and requests:

ich hätte gern ..., ich möchte ...

The imperfect and pluperfect subjunctives are frequently used after conjunctions such as *als* and *als ob.*

The future subjunctive is formed by using the present subjunctive of *werden* plus the infinitive.

---

(8) Translate into English:

1 Die Studenten erklärten, sie seien immer sehr spät ins Bett gegangen.
2 Meine Freundin fragte mich, ob ich Fremdsprachen studieren wolle.
3 Er hat immer gesagt, dass ihm seine Arbeit gefalle.
4 Sie sagte, sie habe zu viel zu tun.
5 Ich möchte ein gutes Zeugnis haben.
6 Es sieht nicht so aus, als ob er Arbeit finden würde.
7 Sie tut nicht so, als wäre sie fleißig.
8 Würden Sie bitte hier unterschreiben?
9 Ich hätte gern einen guten Job.
10 Sie sagten, sie hätten nichts geplant.

Translate into German:
11 I would like to study in Germany.
12 She said that she was happy.
13 They acted as though they loved German.
14 He said the film was really good.
15 They said they saw a wonderful play last week.
16 Would you please sit down?
17 She looked as though she was tired.
18 I said I did not want to work every day.
19 She asked why we did not come to the party.
20 It isn't as if she went out every night.

A2 Grammar: the passive

What you need to know

At A2 Level, you are expected to be familiar with the use of the passive tenses:

> the present passive: *es wird gemacht* = it is being done
> the imperfect passive: *es wurde gemacht* − it was being done
> the perfect passive: *es ist gemacht worden* = it has been done
> the pluperfect passive: *es war gemacht worden* = it had been done
> the future passive: *es wird gemacht werden* = it will be done

NB: with modal verbs, the tense is expressed through the modal verb, and the other verb remains in the passive infinitive: *es muss sofort gemacht werden.*

---

(9) Translate into English:

1 Es wurde ihnen gesagt, dass man schnell etwas tun solle.
2 In der Umweltpolitik wird nicht genug getan.
3 Abwässer von Chemiefabriken wurden oft in den Rhein geleitet.
4 Atomkraft wird in vielen Kraftwerken produziert.
5 Plastiktüten werden mehrmals verwendet.
6 Plastikflaschen wurden durch Glasflaschen ersetzt.
7 Sperrmüll wurde regelmäßig abgeholt.
8 Abfallsünder wurden bestraft.
9 Katalysatoren mussten in Autos eingebaut werden.
10 In vielen Gärten sind schon Komposthaufen angelegt worden.

Translate into German:

11 It will never be done.
12 Glass and metal were collected separately.
13 Pictures of rubbish heaps and the hole in the ozone layer are being shown.
14 Old paper had been collected.
15 Competitions with prizes were organised.
16 Wonderful cloth bags have been produced.
17 The shopping ought to be put in them.
18 The bus has been used more often.
19 The bike cannot be used at the moment.
20 It was damaged in an accident last week.

b, d und g   CD Track 6

Vergleichen Sie:

Bild	o**b**
blei**b**en	schrei**b**t
Deutsch	gesun**d**
dürfen	bal**d**
gut	Ta**g**
ganz	Erfol**g**

Consonants **b, d** and **g** are pronounced like **p, t** and **k** respectively when they appear at the end of a word or in front of **s** or **t**.

Üben Sie jetzt diese Sätze:

Jeden Tag gesund essen – der gute Weg zum Erfolg!
Mein deutscher Freund wird bald kommen.
Ich weiß nicht, ob er lange bleibt.

-ig, -ich, -isch   CD Track 7

Wiederholen Sie die Adjektive:

wen**ig**	mög**lich**	prakt**isch**
bill**ig**	eigent**lich**	polit**isch**
witz**ig**	jugend**lich**	laun**isch**
günst**ig**	schrift**lich**	erfinder**isch**

Versuchen Sie jetzt diesen Zungenbrecher:

Theoretisch ist das richtig, aber eigentlich gar nicht wichtig – beschwichtigt der ewig praktische Herr Derwisch.

s, ß, st, sp   CD Track 8

Üben Sie diese Wörter:

Sonntag	**s**ein
Stein	**Str**aße
Fu**ß**ball	**Sp**aß
Sorge	Pa**ss**
Staatsangehörigkeit	**St**atistik

Zungenbrecher:

Am Sonntag sitzt sein Sohn auf der Straße in der Stadt, sonst strickt er Socken, spielt Fußball und sammelt Steine.

Pronunciation

ei, ie CD Track 9

Wiederholen Sie:

eins, zwei, drei
Eintracht und Zwietracht
Dienstag, Mittwoch und Freitag
schwierig
der Schweiß

Die Arbeit ist nicht schwierig, aber schweißtreibend.
Ich schreibe. Ich schrieb. Ich habe geschrieben.
Er muss sich entscheiden. Er hat sich entschieden.
Liebeslieder von Liebe und Leiden

Lange und kurze Vokale CD Track 10

Wiederholen Sie:

langer Vokal:
mag, Rad, Spaß, Abend, sagen
sehr, gehen, jedes, Federball, Meter
mir, hier, Spiel, Ziel, viel
ohne, wohnen, so, oder, Mode
Ruhe, Schule, Fuß, zu, nun

kurzer Vokal:
hallo, etwas, Geschmack, Stadt, satt
Essen, Tennis, schlecht, Welt, Geld
bist, sich, immer, finden, Wirkung
kommen, besonders, Kosten, gebrochen, noch
muss, Mutter, Eiskunstlauf, Druck, Schuss

Vokale mit Umlaut CD Track 11

Wiederholen Sie:

schön	*erhöht*	*gewöhnlich*	*könnte*
über	*hübsch*	*Grüße*	*müsste*
Ähnlichkeit	*erwähnen*	*Fähigkeit*	*ändern*

Lesen Sie diese Wörter laut. Überprüfen Sie danach die Aussprache.

übertrieben	*Aufklärungsarbeit*	*hören*	*jeder fünfte*	*Gegensätze*
möglich	*Gefühl*	*Schönheitsideal*	*schädlich*	*fünf*
Essstörungen	*gefährlich*	*Öffentlichkeit*	*übermäßig*	*abhängig*

Zungenbrecher:

Der Mondschein schien schon schön.

36

-z und -zw

Wiederholen Sie:

Ziel	Zug	Zaun	Zweig	Zwerg	Zweck
Einzelzimmer	jetzt	zuletzt	kurz	nützlich	
Unterstützung	Sturz	Arzt	zwanzig	gezwungen	zwölf

Hören Sie zu und wiederholen Sie:

jetzt – zuletzt
zu zweit – Zeit
kurz – Sturz
zwanzig – Zwetschgen
Zweck – Zecke

Probieren Sie diese Sätze:

Setzen Sie sich in den Zug.
Zwischen zwölf und zwei.
Zieh jetzt kurz am Seil.
Zwei Ziegen sitzen vor dem Zaun.

Zungenbrecher:

Zwischen zwei Zelten zwitschern zwölf Zaunkönige.

Compound words

Wiederholen Sie:

a Gleich/geschlechtliche Partnerschaften
b Lebens/abschnitts/gefährte
c Wieder/heirat
d Geschäfts/reise
e auseinander/brechen
f Kinder/tages/stätte
g Wieder/vereinigung
h Gehirn/masse
i Wohn/gemeinschaft
j Abenteuer/lust

Unit 1 Ausländer

der Ausländer	foreigner
der Aussiedler	resettler
der Gastarbeiter	guest worker
der Asylbewerber	asylum seeker
das Herkunftsland	country of origin
der Einwanderer	immigrant
der Auswanderer	emigrant
der Antrag	application
verfolgt	persecuted
integrieren	integrate
der Bürger	citizen
die Einbürgerung	citizenship
die Aufenthaltserlaubnis	residence permit
die Arbeitsgenehmigung	work permit
die Familie nachholen	to bring one's family over
sich einleben	to settle down
unqualifizierte Arbeit	unskilled work
schlecht bezahlt	poorly paid
niedrig	menial
ablehnen	to reject
die kulturelle Indentität wahren	to maintain cultural identity
Angst haben (vor)	to be afraid
die Ungleichheit	inequality
der Rassismus	racism
die Rassendiskriminierung	racial discrimination
die Ausländerfeindlichkeit	xenophobia, dislike of foreigners
der Neonazismus	neo-Nazism
der kulturelle Konflikt	cultural clash
verschlimmern/verbessern	to get worse/to improve
der Sündenbock	scapegoat
die Rassenkonflikte	racial tensions
die Gewalt	violence
die Rassenunruhen	riots
die Feindseligkeit	hostility
fremd	foreign
der gegenseitige Respekt	mutual respect
die Toleranz	tolerance
die kulturelle Vielfalt	cultural diversity
zweisprachig	bilingual

Unit 2 Rechtswesen und Verbrechen

die Gewalt	violence
tatverdächtig sein	to be suspected (of a crime)
das Delikt(e)	crime
verurteilt	convicted
der Straftäter	criminal
die Straftat	crime

der Ladendiebstahl	shoplifting
die Sachbeschädigung	criminal damage
Schwarzfahren	fare dodging
die Körperverletzung	physical injury
anzeigen	to press charges
begehen	commit
benachrichtigen	to report
das Verbrechen	crime
der Diebstahl	theft
die Gewalttat	crime of violence
das Gerichtsverfahren	court hearing
der Betrug	fraud, scam
das Betäubungsmittel	narcotic
die Strafverfolgungsbehörde	law enforcement agency
erforderlich	necessary, essential
verführen	to seduce
verboten	forbidden
illegal	illegal
vorsichtig	careful
misstrauisch	suspicious
verlockend	alluring, tempting
die Gefängnisstrafe	prison sentence
das Gefängnis	prison
die Todesstrafe	death penalty
die Abschreckung	deterrent
das Opfer	victim
die Überwachungskamera	security camera

Unit 3 Armut und Reichtum

die Armut	poverty
das Elend	misery
die Armutsgrenze	poverty threshold
die Kluft	gap
der Reichtum	riches
der Obdachlose	homeless person
obdachlos	homeless
arbeitslos/die Arbeitslosigkeit	unemployed/unemployment
betteln	to beg
der Bettler	beggar
die Herberge	hostel
die Dritte Welt	the Third World
die Sozialhilfe	social services
die Entwicklungsländer	developing countries
die Unterernährung	malnutrition
die Hungersnot	famine
die Dürre	drought
die Infektionskrankheiten	infectious diseases
der Krieg	war

die Katastrophe	disaster
das Erdbeben	earthquake
die medizinische Fürsorge	medical/health care
teilen	to share
Probleme lösen	to solve problems
die Ausbildung anregen	to encourage schooling
fairer Handel	fair trade
von seiner Arbeit leben	to live from one's work
die Ausbeutung	exploitation
die Biobaumwolle	organic cotton
das anständige Gehalt	fair pay
die Gleichberechtigung	equality
das Wohlwollen	goodwill
die Grundrechte	basic rights
die moralischen Werte	ethical values
der Wohlfahrtsverband	charity
fördern	(to) support
freiwillig	voluntary

Unit 4 Umweltverschmutzung

die Umwelt	the environment
der Umweltschutz	environmental conservation
der Treibhauseffekt	greenhouse effect
die Energiekrise	the energy crisis
der Energiebedarf	energy need
der Sonnenkollektor(-en)	a solar panel
die Sonnenenergie/der Solarstrom	solar energy
die Energiequelle	source of energy
das Windrad	wind turbine
die Atomenergie	nuclear power
das Kernkraftwerk	nuclear power station
belasten	to pollute
verpesten	to pollute
schaden	to damage
verschwenden	to waste
vergiften	to poison
gefährden	to endanger
erschöpft werden	to run out
die Entwaldung	deforestation
die Erwärmung der Erdatmosphäre	global warming
die Überschwemmung	flood
der Orkan(-e)	hurricane
schmelzen	to melt
der Säuregehalt	level of acidity
der Meeresspiegel	ocean level
die Ursache	cause
die Auswirkung	effect

der Klimawandel	climate change
der Gletscher	glacier

Unit 5 Umweltschutz

umweltfreundlich	environmentally friendly
umweltfeindlich	damaging to the environment
schützen	to protect
das Umweltbewusstsein	environmental awareness
die Umwelterziehung	environmental education
die Schadstoffbelastung mindern	to reduce damage by pollutants
retten	to save
die Bedrohung der Menschen	threat to humanity
die dauerhafte Entwicklung	sustainable development
demonstrieren/eine Demonstration	to demonstrate/a demonstration
verbessern	to improve
das Benehmen ändern	to change the behaviour
die Ausstellung	exhibition
kämpfen gegen	to fight against
der Gegner	activist
das Licht ausschalten	to put out the light
die Heizung herunterdrehen	to turn down the heating
die Fahrgemeinschaft	car-sharing
Müll trennen	(to separate) household rubbish
der Sperrmüll	bulky rubbish
recyceln/das Recycling	to recycle/recycling
die Industrieländer	the industrialised countries
alternative Energiequellen	alternative energy sources
entwickeln	to develop
die Plastiktüte	plastic bag
biologisch abbaubar	biodegradable
vernichten	to destroy
das Benzin	petrol
das Rohöl	crude oil
die Kohle	coal
der Energieverbrauch	energy consumption
der Brennstoff	fuel
der Wasserstoff	hydrogen
der Sauerstoff	oxygen
das Kohlendioxid	carbon dioxide CO_2

Unit 6 Technik und die Zukunft

die neue Technologie	new technology
genetisch	genetic
die Gentechnik	genetic engineering
das Klonen/klonen	cloning/to clone
entdecken	to discover
gentechnisch verändert	genetically modified
genmanipuliert	genetically modified

Vocabulary

das Erbgut	genetic make-up
das Gen	gene
erfinden/die Erfindung	to invent/invention
die Zeitreise	time travel
die Reise begrenzen	to limit the journey
im Internet einkaufen	to shop on the Internet
der Fortschritt	progress
ein defektes Gen	a defective gene
eine erblich bedingte Fehlsteuerung	a congenital disorder
die Erbkrankheit	.hereditary illness
heilen	to cure
ethische Bedenken	ethical considerations
die Transplantation	transplant
das Retortenbaby	test-tube baby
der Embryo	embryo
der DNS-Code	DNA code
der Spender	donor
die Lebensqualität	quality of life
verbessern	to improve
entwickeln	to develop
Wirklichkeit werden	to become reality
forschen über	to research into
die Forschung	research
das Reagenzglas	test tube
die embryonale Stammzelle	embryonic stem cell
ausgestorben	extinct

Unit 7 Literatur, Film und die bildende Kunst

die Schönheit	beauty
die Wahrheit	truth
der Geschmack	taste
schildern	to depict
der Leser	the reader
eine Geschichte erzählen	to tell a story
in anderen Sprachen übersetzt	translated into other languages
das Drehbuch	screenplay
einen Film drehen	to make a film
der Handwerker	craftsman
der Dichter	poet
das Gedicht	poem
der Regisseur	director
der Roman	novel
der Künstler	artist
der Schriftsteller	writer
das Stück	play
der Titel	title
düster	bleak

die Hauptfigur	main character
die Regie	direction
die Anerkennung	recognition
der Kassenerfolg	box-office success
die Kritik	review
der Schauplatz	scene
der Schauspieler	actor
der Hauptdarsteller	principal actor
die Landschaft	landscape
das Mitglied	member
entdeckt	discovered
der Schwarzmarkt	black market
der Maler	painter
das Motiv	theme
das Werk	work
zu Lebzeiten	when alive
das Gemälde	painting
der Architekt	architect

Unit 8 Politik – Globale Probleme

die Globalisierung	globalisation
die Regierung	government
der Staat	state
die Wirtschaftsmacht	economic power
der Weltmarkt	world market
wettbewerbsfähig	competitive
die Demokratie	democracy
die Macht	power
das Recht	the right
versammeln	to assemble, congregate
rechtsextremistisch	right-wing
der Krieg	war
der Frieden	peace
beherrschen	rule
der Angriff	attack
der Drahtzieher	manipulator
der Attentäter	assassin
der Terrorverdächtige	terrorist suspect
vereitelt	thwarted
der Bundestag	German parliament
der Eiserne Vorhang	Iron Curtain
die Ölkrise	oil crisis
der Abbau	phasing out
Terrorismus bekämpfen	to combat terrorism
stimmen für/gegen	to vote for/against
die Wahl	election
die Stimme	the vote

Vocabulary

Unit 9 Deutschland heute

die Mauer	wall
die Teilung	separation
die Wende	turning point
die Wiedervereinigung	reunification
Ossis	people from East Germany
Wessis	people from West Germany
die EU	European Union
der Euro	euro
die Muttersprache	mother tongue
die Wirtschaft	economy
das Wirtschaftswachstum	economic growth
das Zusammengehörigkeitsgefühl	feeling of belonging
die Mitgliedstaaten (pl)	member states
deutschsprachig	German speaking

1

1 We must use cooler water in the washing machine.
2 Forest exploitation shows no respect for nature.
3 We expect better next time!
4 Carbon gas has the worst effect on our atmosphere.
5 We have no more realistic solutions.
6 What should we do to find the right road?
7 The transport system of the future will be much more efficient.
8 A varied diet is better for health.
9 I am clearly more optimistic than you are.
10 The sun is a direct source of light and heat.
11 Züge sind umweltfreundlicher als Autos.
12 Wir haben genug Erdgas, aber kein Benzin.
13 Ein altes Auto ist nicht gut für die Umwelt.
14 Ein neues Auto ist genauso schlimm wie ein altes.
15 Ihr Haus hat Sonnenkollektoren.
16 Meine Zentralheizung ist teuer.
17 Es gibt eine gute Atmosphäre im Ökodorf.
18 Dort wohnen die Leute billiger als bei uns.
19 Recyceln Sie (Recycelst du) alte Zeitungen und leere Flaschen?
20 Welche Energie ist am billigsten?

2

1 Immigrants? Do we pay them child benefit?
2 According to German law, no one can be disadvantaged because of their race.
3 Immigrants came to Germany with their families.
4 In the last hundred years, German re-settlers have suffered much because of their nationality.
5 We all have the right to the nationality of the country in which we are born.
6 Immigrants came to work in our country.
7 We stand against anyone who doesn't respect human rights.
8 Germany is the country in which I grew up and whose culture I try to adapt to.
9 I am not allowed to forget my origins.
10 We are regarded as belonging to nowhere.
11 Erklären Sie (Erkläre) mir, was Rassismus bedeutet.
12 Ich habe ihnen gesagt, dass ich sie nicht verstehe.
13 Er wohnt jetzt in Leipzig und findet die Stadt sehr ruhig.
14 Das ist eine Stadt, die ich nicht kenne.
15 Gastarbeiter sind hauptsächlich Türken, die zum Arbeiten nach Deutschland gekommen sind.
16 Die Aussiedler sind Deutsche, die in Osteuropa jetzt wohnen.
17 Sie wohnen dort seit 20 Jahren.
18 Die Karte? Zeigen Sie (Zeig) sie mir, bitte.
19 Die Ausländerfeindlichkeit – was ist die Ursache davon?
20 Wir müssen versuchen, sie mit Toleranz zu ersetzen.

3

1 How do you solve these problems?
2 Do you already do something to raise money for a charity?
3 What do such charities need in order to be able to function?
4 We must find a long-term solution.
5 Without a job, you cannot pay the rent.
6 Without accommodation it is difficult to find a job
7 We try to help these people to rebuild their society.
8 The Third World countries should be allowed to forget their debts to the industrial countries.
9 We must not forget that all people need help.
10 When you live in absolute poverty, you do not have enough to eat.
11 Jeder sollte einen bestimmten Lebensstandard haben.
12 Arbeitest du/Arbeiten Sie bei einer Wohlfahrtsorganisation?
13 Ich will anderen Leuten helfen, eine Zukunft zu haben.
14 In vielen Ländern können viele Leute weder schreiben noch lesen.
15 Ich hoffe, ihnen helfen zu können.
16 Sie will nach Afrika gehen, um dort den Kindern zu helfen.
17 Wir arbeiten dort schon seit zehn Jahren.
18 Das Leben kann für allein erziehende Mütter sehr schwierig sein.
19 Viele junge Leute wollen reich sein.
20 Was macht man, wenn man keinen Job finden kann?

4

1 The poet Johann Wolfgang von Goethe was born in 1749.
2 Karl Wilhelm Gropius trained as a landscape painter in Berlin.
3 In this era, society was dominated by men.
4 Fassbinder was born in 1945 and spent his childhood in a chaotic post-war Germany.
5 Marlene Dietrich went to school in Berlin and Dessau.
6 In April 1930, she left Germany and emigrated to America.
7 Roland Emmerich began his career as a film director in Germany.
8 Later he found fame in America.
9 Wim Wenders' first successful film was 'Paris, Texas' (1984).
10 His 1987 film 'Wings of Desire' inspired the 1998 film 'City of Angels' with Meg Ryan and Nicholas Cage.
11 Wie viele Leute haben das Pergamonmuseum im Jahr 2007 besucht?
12 Letztes Jahr wurde dieses Bild für $78 000 000 verkauft.
13 Christa Wolf wurde 1929 geboren.
14 Sie glaubte nicht an die Auflösung der DDR.
15 Lessing studierte zuerst Medizin und Theologie in Leipzig.
16 Danach lebte er als Schriftsteller in Berlin, wo er für mehrere Zeitungen schrieb.
17 1995 gewann Franka Potente den Bayerischen Filmpreis als beste Nachwuchsschauspielerin.
18 Tom Tykwer schrieb die Rolle der Lola im Film ‚Lola rennt' für sie.
19 Franka Potente hat auch ein Drehbuch geschrieben.
20 Annette von Droste-Hülshoff schrieb schöne Balladen und Gedichte über Westfalen.

5

1 Tomorrow we will live in a world full of computers.
2 In the future, computers will help you get everything done.
3 It will no longer be necessary to leave the house, for you will have everything you need at home.
4 Scientists' decisions will have serious consequences.
5 Because of genetics, it will be possible to cure many hereditary illnesses.
6 But there will be no miracle cure in the next five years.
7 Genetic manipulation could create a world full of perfect people.
8 All food will be genetically modified.
9 Genetically modified food could cause new allergies.
10 If you knew that such food was harmless, you could solve the food problems of the developing countries with it.
11 Wie werden wir in der Zukunft leben?
12 Es wird überall Computer geben.
13 Wir werden im Internet einkaufen.
14 Man wird seinen Urlaub auf dem Mond verbringen können.
15 Wie wird das tägliche Leben aussehen?
16 Mein Computer wird mir helfen, Entscheidungen zu treffen.
17 Die Wissenschaftler werden sehr verantwortungsvoll sein müssen.
18 Ich möchte nicht in einer perfekten Welt wohnen.
19 Man sollte mehr über Technologie wissen.
20 Wenn ich jung wäre, würde ich Informatik studieren.

6

1 We must not forget that cultural diversity is very important in Europe.
2 Don't be afraid of the European Union!
3 For the moment, the EU has neither president nor soldiers.
4 We have never been to Germany.
5 I am not afraid of losing my identity.
6 Old people will no longer be isolated but respected and valued.
7 Not only has the EU good ideas for the future but also concrete proposals to finance these ideas.
8 Europe has nothing to hide.
9 Not all EU members want the euro.
10 The global economy has no confidence in the European politicians.
11 Ist Polen kein EU-Mitglied?
12 Er hatte nicht gewählt.
13 Du wirst (Sie werden) Russland nie besuchen.
14 Die EU ist nicht mehr klein.
15 Ich möchte nicht EU-Präsident sein!
16 Ich habe keinen Pass mehr.
17 Nichts ist sicherer.
18 Ich habe keinen einzigen Euro übrig.
19 Ich verbringe meine Ferien lieber nicht in Europa.
20 Ich habe weder die Zeit noch das Geld.

(7)

1 Of course she was pleased when she got good marks.
2 Many women choose to work part-time when they have children.
3 He did not work much in school, but he works very hard now in his apprenticeship.
4 She is studying in Germany because she can speak German very well.
5 Because she wants to work in a bank, she hopes to study maths at university.
6 Marlene Dietrich emigrated to America because she hated the Nazis.
7 "Run, Lola, Run" is the story of a woman who wants to save her boyfriend.
8 Berlin is a beautiful city with lots of history.
9 Because they speak different languages in Switzerland, it is a complicated country.
10 Brandenburg is one of the new federal counties which used to be a part of the GDR.
11 Letztes Jahr habe ich an der Universität Bremen studiert.
12 Viele junge Leute sprechen sehr gut Fremdsprachen, und deshalb können sie überall in der EU einen Job finden.
13 Sie interessierte sich nicht für große Filme, sondern wollte außergewöhnliche Geschichten erzählen.
14 Es hat Anne Frank sehr gefallen, als Leute sie besucht haben.
15 Die Stasizeit war sehr schlimm, weil man jedem misstraute.
16 Die Nazizeit war genauso schlimm, da jeder Angst hatte.
17 Da die Westberliner nicht mehr nach Ostberlin durften, konnten viele Leute nicht zur Arbeit gehen.
18 Man hat die Mauer gebaut, weil viele Ostdeutsche das Land verlassen wollten.
19 Westberlin war sehr isoliert, weil es nur eine Zufahrt dahin gab.
20 Marlene Dietrich wurde 1901 in Berlin geboren.

(8)

1 The students explained that they always went to bed very late.
2 My friend asked me if I wanted to study languages.
3 He always said he liked his work.
4 She said she had too much to do.
5 I would like a good report.
6 It does not look as though he will find work.
7 She does not act as if she were hardworking.
8 Would you please sign here?
9 I would like a good job.
10 They said they had nothing planned.
11 Ich möchte in Deutschland studieren.
12 Sie sagte, sie sei glücklich.
13 Sie benahmen sich, als ob sie Deutsch geliebt hätten.
14 Er sagte, der Film sei wirklich gut.